# Contents

**page**

## Say the sounds

j v w y z ch sh th ng

# The animal park

We had a visit to an animal park with Mum.

My job was to look at the map.

It was a big park, with lots of animals to see.

Look at this zebra go!

The zebras ran in the park.

This animal hid in the park.

This animal fed in the park.

neck

Can he get to the top?

# Big cats

We ran to see the big cats.

Fizz had cubs.

cubs

# Chimps

We had fun looking at the chimps.

The dad chimp got mad with his kids!

# Panda

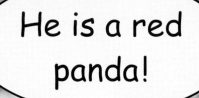

He is a red panda!

We had fun looking for the panda! He hid for a nap.

# At the end

fish

At the end of the visit, we ran to see the animals get fed.

Then Mum fed us!

It was a fun visit.

# Index